BATMAN

KIDS COLOURING BOOK

YOUNG WRITERS GROUP

Contents

Acknowledgements

THIS BOOK IS SPECIALLY DESIGNED AND MADE FOR CHILDREN'S LEARNING WITH ENJOYMENT .
IT CONTRIBUTES TO VARIOUS COLOURING CHARACTER AND KNOWLEDGE FOR YOUR GROWING CHILD.
IT PROVIDES OPPORTUNITY TO LEARN VARIOUS LEARNING BENEFITS.
THIS BOOK CONTAINS VARIOUS ADORABLE AND GORGEOUS CHARACTERS FOR YOUR CHILD'S ENLIGHTMENT.
Colouring books provide an opportunity for children to not only colour in but also various other learning benefits.
'365 Colouring Book', this gorgeous book contains adorable designs that kids will definitely love.
TEAM YOUNG WRITERS GROUP.

CHAPTER ONE

BATMAN

BATMAN

BAT MAN

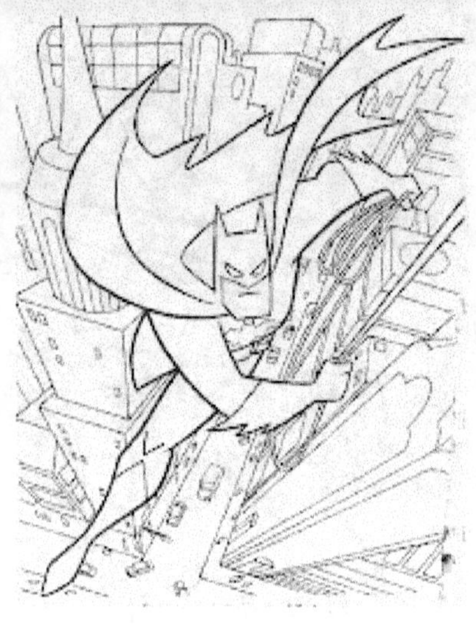

Ywg.official

Young Writers Group (YWG.OFFICIAL) is an organisation which is working to help writers in showcasing their work in front of vast number of readers . We offers a budget friendly packages to our writers. We are working as a writer's helping society. You can have a talk with us regarding publishing your book on our instagram
:@YWG.OFFICIAL
Or you can drop your mail on ywg.co.in@gmail.com
Else you can also contact us on following numbers
Akash: 7404390981
Aashika: 9634644516